Herald Express

Nine Short Pub Walks
in and around
TORBAY

Brian Carter

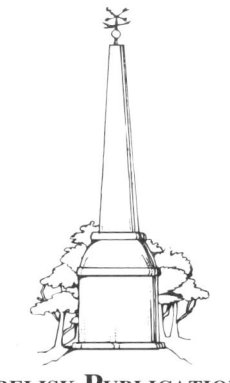

OBELISK PUBLICATIONS

ALSO BY THE AUTHOR
Walks in The South Hams
Pub Walks in the South Hams
Pub Walks in and around The Haldon Hills
OTHER BOOKS ABOUT TORBAY AND SOUTH DEVON
Torbay in Colour–Torquay, Paignton, Brixham, *Chips Barber*
The Ghosts of Torbay, *Deryck Seymour*
Under Sail through South Devon & Dartmoor, *Raymond B Cattell*
The Great Little Totnes Book, *Chips Barber*
Torquay, *Chips Barber*
Paignton, *Chips Barber*
Brixham, *Chips Barber*

We have over 150 Devon-based titles – for a list of current books please write to us at
2 Church Hill, Pinhoe, Exeter, EX4 9ER telephone (01392) 468556

Acknowledgements
All sketch maps, based on out-of-copyright sources, by Brian Carter
All drawings by Brian Carter
All photographs by Chips Barber

Front Cover photo was taken in the grounds behind Torre Abbey
Back Cover is the view towards Teignmouth from Babbacombe Downs

First published in 1997 by
Obelisk Publications, 2 Church Hill, Pinhoe, Exeter, Devon
Designed by Chips and Sally Barber
Typeset by Sally Barber
Printed in Great Britain by
The Devonshire Press Ltd, Torquay, Devon

© **Brian Carter/Obelisk Publications 1997**
All Rights Reserved. No part of this publication may be reproduced, stored in a retrieval system, or transmitted, in any form or by any means, electronic, mechanical, photocopying, recording or otherwise, without the prior permission of the publishers and copyright holders.

CONTENTS

1: "To The Lyte House" … page 4
2: Fine Woodland and Larksong … page 9
3: Eating, Walking and Being Merry … page 11
4: Lanes, Meadows and Ale … page 14
5: Proms, Sugar and Bogart … page 17
6: Serenaded by the Grasshopper Chorus … page 21
7: Seaside Cappuccino but no sign of Bardot … page 23
8: Walking Down into the Valley of the Rocks … page 26
9: Up on the Downs … page 30

1: "TO THE LYTE HOUSE"

IT WAS a green, sunny day when I came down the lane by the Visitors' Centre at the entrance to Berry Head Country Park car park. The meadow on the left was full of wild flowers and a blackbird was singing across the chalet roofs of the holiday camp.

Round the bend, in Gillard Road, the tall hedge of ash, hawthorn, hazel and blackthorn was crowded with sparrow fledglings and cow parsley nodded in the sea breeze, but I didn't see any of those rare little songbirds, the cirl buntings, which live in the seaside fields.

At the crossroads I turned left into Sea Lane and walked down to pick up the coast path for another left turn. Then it was good to vault the stile and wander across the first of the clifftop meadows. The rabbits didn't trust me, though, and legged it into the brambles as I loped along the rough track with just butterflies, hoverflies and bumble bees for company.

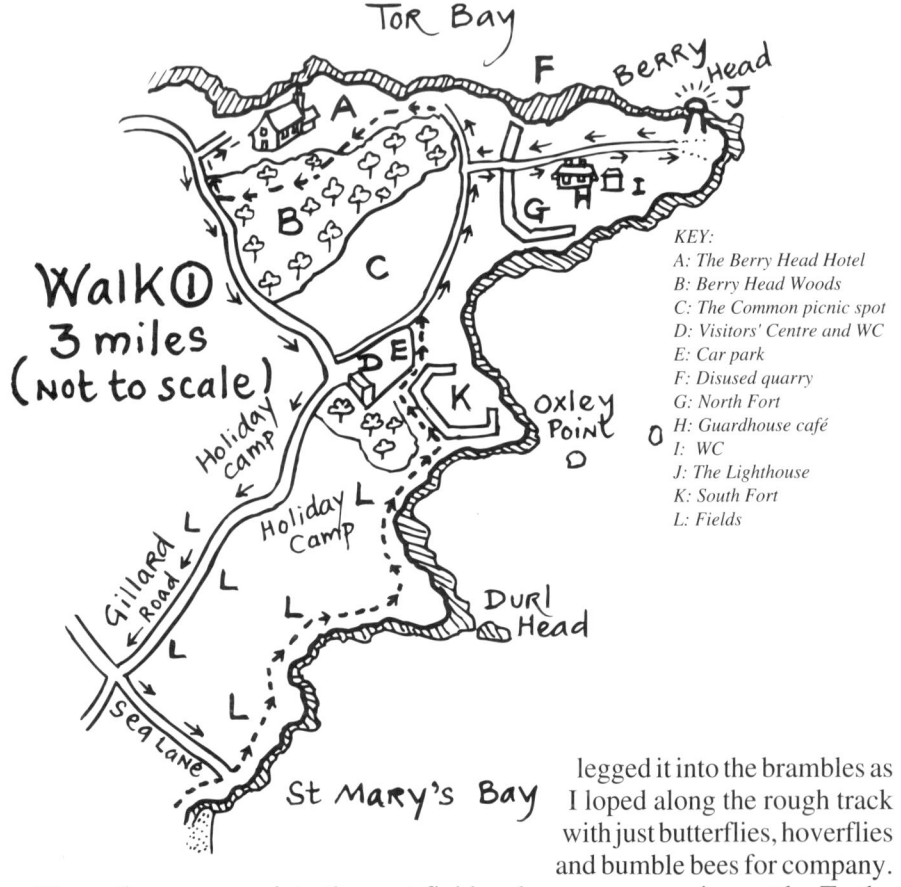

Walk ①
3 miles
(not to scale)

KEY:
A: The Berry Head Hotel
B: Berry Head Woods
C: The Common picnic spot
D: Visitors' Centre and WC
E: Car park
F: Disused quarry
G: North Fort
H: Guardhouse café
I: WC
J: The Lighthouse
K: South Fort
L: Fields

The path saw me up into the next field and on among grazing cattle. To the right the blue English Channel met the blue sky on an horizon lost in haze. And soon I was climbing a stone stile, which had a hole for dogs, to drop onto the path and stroll to Durl Head.

There the jackdaws' aerial cabaret, and the views back across St Mary's Bay to Sharkham Point, were the sort of bonuses any hikers worth their salt would have appreciated.

Another stone stile later and I was beside the wild-flower meadow that had caught my eye when I left the car park. Among the buttercups and sorrel were the pink flowers of common centaury, and on the turf slope near the South Fort some of Berry Head's white rock-roses were catching the sun.

Now the path ran above the dry moat under the fort's ramparts to Berry Head car park where the walk had begun. Across the way was the common and picnic area, with its tables, and under the South Fort, to the right, were the breeding ledges of the largest guillemot colony on the South Coast. Upwards of 1,000 birds, known locally as the Brixham penguins, have been recorded on the cliffs.

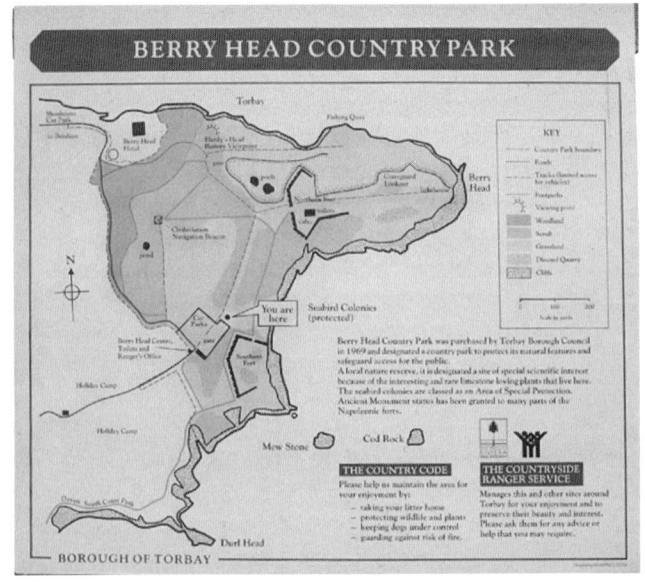

But Berry Head isn't just another Site of Special Scientific Interest. It's a Nature Reserve of national importance, a great limestone 'mausoleum' packed with the remains of a geological age so distant the mind boggles trying to come to terms with it.

The country park has a wealth of wildlife and more than 600 species of flowers. From the common to the woods and cliffs you can see foxes, snakes, all sorts of seabirds, and greater or lesser horseshoe bats leaving the caves in the disused quarry. But there are other attractions, like Marjory's warm apple cake which she serves with a generous dollop of Devonshire clotted cream at her Guardhouse Café in the North Fort.

The fort was the Berry Head base of soldiers during the Napoleonic War. Before that it was an Iron Age fort which the Romans improved during their occupation.

At the end of the headland I had a look at Britain's highest and lowest lighthouse. How come, you may ask. Well, it's nearly 200 feet above the sea, but the actual building is only 15 feet high.

On the edge of the cliffs I found great views of the Channel and Tor Bay, with the Dartmoor hills beyond the heights of Paignton. It was this distant vision of the moorland tors, seen by vessels coming in from the sea, which gave Tor Bay its name.

Retracing my steps I put the North Fort behind me, came right, past the old quarry, and on down the dusty, stony track to the viewpoint complete with its information board which describes the sort of shipping you can see in Tor Bay.

Soon the path deserted the clifftops and wound through the woods to the single track road near Berry Head Cottages. Bearing right, I came down to the Berry Head Hotel with a thirst like the devil's at the end of a hot coals tutorial for lost souls.

The hotel is a kind of stately home on the edge of the cliffs, but the family atmosphere in the Lyte Lounge Bar couldn't be friendlier. Lyte is the giveaway word if you know your great British hymns.

The hotel was built in the infant years of the 19th century, as a hospital for the fort garrison on Berry Head. Then in 1833 it was let to the Rev Henry Francis Lyte, clergyman of Brixham's All Saints Church. He wrote several hymns, including 'Praise, my Soul, the King of Heaven' but his most famous was the words for 'Abide with Me'.

It's believed they were written in the grounds of the Berry Head Hotel in the Autumn of 1847 when he was dying of TB. This is entirely feasible if you've ever sat on the hotel's terrace in the evening and watched a Dartmoor sunset. Torbay has a lot to offer but this is a truly moving experience.

The Rev Lyte died in Nice in November 1847, but 'Abide with Me' is his memorial, and the hymn is part of the fabric of the Berry Head Hotel and the nation's spiritual culture.

It was lunchtime, though, when I arrived in need of a cool pint of Kilkenny. The lounge bar windows offered a marvellous view of the bay and those far-off Dartmoor hills, but I had to go onto the terrace to look down on the fishing boat putting to sea from Brixham.

If the weather had been cool, I would have settled for the bar, which has an open fire, comfortable settees and armchairs and the sort of service you get when the proprietors live on the premises.

Anyway, after my modest lunchtime session I came up the road past Berry Head Cottages, Berry Head Farm (which isn't a farm any more), to the Common and car park, glad I had got the Lighthouse and the Lyte House under my belt yet again.

2: FINE WOODLAND AND LARKSONG

THERE wasn't a cloud in the sky as I left Ye Olde Churston Inn on the edge of the village of Churston Ferrers before noon.

It was one of those classic seaside summer days which Torbay often conjures up to the envy of holiday resorts elsewhere.

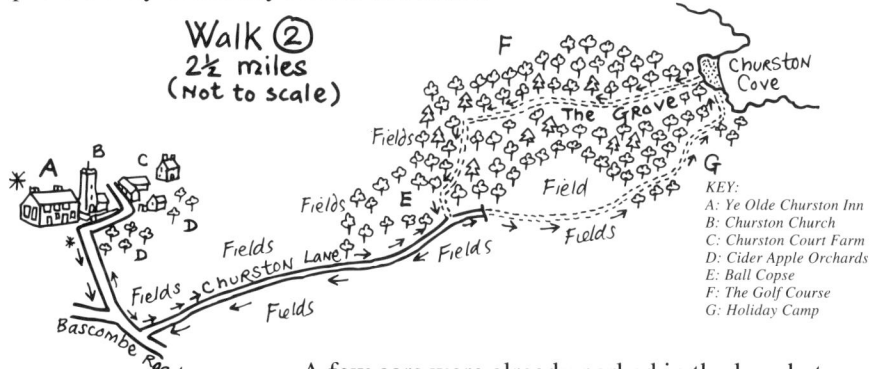

Walk ②
2½ miles
(Not to scale)

KEY:
A: Ye Olde Churston Inn
B: Churston Church
C: Churston Court Farm
D: Cider Apple Orchards
E: Ball Copse
F: The Golf Course
G: Holiday Camp

A few cars were already parked in the lane between the up-market country pub and Bascombe Road. Flickering over the cider apple orchards and churchyard, the swallows of Churston Court Farm celebrated the beauty of the morning on the wing.

Where the lane and busy Bascombe Road met I kept close to the hedge, but for once no cars passed me and I made it to Churston Lane a few yards away with no feathers ruffled by speeding traffic. Then nature took over.

Throughout the year larksong is a major feature of this walk, and I expected the birds to be trilling over the neighbouring fields. But that melodious warbling, as the skylarks rise and fall on their song, always takes me by surprise – a bit like a smile from a girl you're in love with.

Tall hedges, wildflower-rich banks, a gateway view across the combe towards Churston Court Farm, dog roses in bloom – the lane had everything a rural romantic could ask for on a country walk. The fields were small, with hedges mainly of hawthorn, or drystone walls, and lots of songbirds and their fledgelings were using the lane as an insect takeaway.

Towards the bottom of the combe stood Ball Copse with the more extensive woodland of The Grove meeting it farther on. Then I came through a gate where Churston Lane ended and a footpath ran across a big, weedy meadow. To the left and ahead were the trees of The Grove, and the patch of common before I entered the wood was sprinkled with rabbit droppings.

Someone had switched off the larksong and I was coming down the steps under ash and sycamore, passing the holiday camp chalets before turning left at the Churston Cove signpost.

Soon the descent became steeper and the steps wider, bringing me into the sight, sound and smell of the sea. After the old farmland that view of Tor Bay, the end of Brixham Breakwater, and the hills of Torquay, was the sort of thing that makes walks memorable.

Although I was dressed in shorts, T-shirt and trainers some of last night's vintage cider and Irish whiskey was leaking from my pores by the time I had negotiated the rocky section above the low seacliffs. Then it was a relief to crunch onto the pebbly little beach at Churston Cove for a much needed paddle.

Behind the cove the footpath cut back into The Grove again, taking me between slopes covered with trees, including some huge sweet chestnuts. Over the years I've bumped into foxes, badgers, a stoat or two, and other wild creatures on this trail. But high noon on a summer day, with other walkers and their dogs about, is not the best time to play nature detective.

The grey squirrels were aloft doing their treetop gymnastics and maybe lunching on a few unlucky fledgelings. But it was good to find the third belt of larches had been felled *en route* to the fork, where I came left up the steps and out of The Grove into Churston Lane once more to reverse the first part of the walk.

One of Torbay's largest woods, The Grove has some fine ash and oaks, as well as these majestic chestnuts. Under them, if you come at the right time of year, you'll see plants like the early purple orchid, wood spurge, goldilocks and bluebells. And among the resident birds are green woodpeckers and great spotted woodpeckers – so if you have a wooden head wear a helmet!

Back at Ye Olde Churston Inn I found the owner strolling around the grounds with his big Old English Mastiffs Ethelred and Athelstan.

The inn, formerly Churston Court, has three large gardens open to the public, and is ideal for groups of friends and families. You can take the sun and enjoy a drink, a snack or a larger meal at a picnic table. "Hospitality is high on our priority list," he told me as we went inside. Well, the old Manor House has a lot of history in its warm atmosphere, which the staff have worked hard to create.

All the rooms are special to say the least, with a baronial bar, huge open fires, high ceilings, a restaurant, carvery, mediaeval music and a resident ghost. As pubs go it has a rich aristocratic edge to it, but it's nice to hear my own redsoil Devon accent when locals gather. The food is good and I settled for a glass of cider and cheese sandwiches in the sunlit top garden, where a blackbird provided the sort of serenade money can't buy.

3: EATING, WALKING AND BEING MERRY

LATE one morning I set off from the main car park in Cockington. The heart of the village was just down the road on the left, where a couple of the horse-drawn carriages were waiting to take holidaymakers on rides through the country park.

In front of me was Rose Cottage, with its fish pond and tea garden, to the left was the Old School House gift shop, and over on the right were the Forge and The Old Granary gift and craft shop. It was sunshine, thatch and more thatch, great cream teas, coveys of foreign visitors and lots of old-world country charm.

I came down Cockington Lane past the cider apple orchard, some barn conversions and a stream with ducks on it. Lanscombe House tempted with its cream teas and a little later my route was signposted on the right: The Lakes and Gamekeeper's Cottage. So that's the way I went, under the arch at Lower Lodge. Shrubs were in flower, birds sang and at the first of the three ponds I said goodbye to the main path and walked the footpath on the left below Hellinghay Wood.

Walk 3
3 miles
(not to scale)

KEY:
A: The Drum Inn
B: Car park, Information Centre, toilets
C: The Mill Café
D: Old Granary gift shop
E: The Old School House shop
F: Rose Cottage Tea Garden
G: The Forge
H: Lanscombe House Tea Garden and Café
I: Lower Lodge
J: The Ponds
K: Hellinghay Wood
L: The Gamekeeper's Cottage
M: Manscombe Woods
N: Warren Barn
O: Cockington Church
P: The Organic Garden
Q: Cockington Court
R: Dew Park
S: Old Cider Press
T: Cockington Park
U: Higher Lodge
V: To Torquay Seafront
W: Old Paignton Road

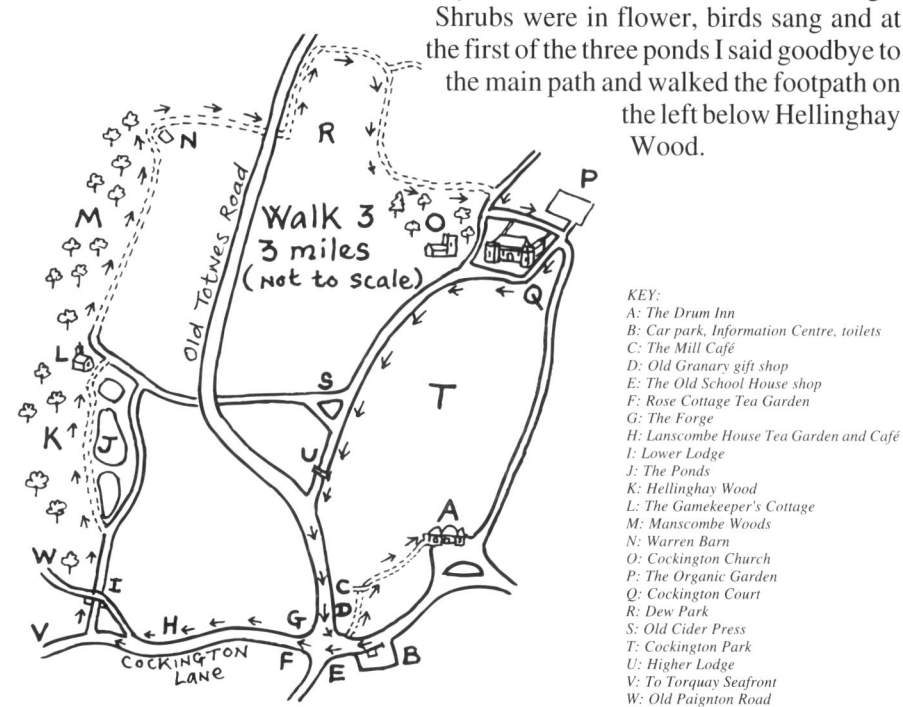

Big ghostly carp were rolling on the surface of the middle pond as I came by. Insects clung to the huge green leaves of gunnera, which I've always called Elephant Ear Rhubarb. Then I was passing the Gamekeeper's Cottage on the left, to swing right and come along the edge of Manscombe Wood to Warren Barn, where I turned right beyond the gate to walk the footpath in the combe.

At the top I crossed Old Totnes Road and followed the bridle-path left above Dew Park and views of Cockington Valley.

It was a countryside of small fields, drystone walls and bushy hedges with wild flowers at their feet. Old trees stood here and there in the wide green spaces and I bore right at the big ash tree where the signpost read: Cockington Court.

Then I made an abrupt right-turn at the hazel hedge and walked the redsoil footpath with foxgloves each side of it. Two stiles later I was behind Cockington Church.

At the 'crossroads' I turned right before bearing left to come through the gate and on beyond the stables to the Organic Garden up on the left.

If all this twisting and turning sounds confusing, believe me, it isn't. The footpaths are carefully signposted and even the local cider gnomes, in their apple-drugged state, rarely get lost.

The Organic Garden is a must when it comes to Cockington browse-abouts. Apart from the wide variety of good, wholesome vegetables growing there, you'll find a dragonfly pond, an apiary buzzing with bees, compost heaps and a wormery.

Leaving the garden the route was straight ahead past the rural craft HQ in the old stables to the front of Cockington Court. Here the sweeping view of the park, with its cricket field and trees, is idyllic in the English rural tradition.

There's lots to see inside the Court where the café, craft shop and bakery are always busy. The bakery is where I come for my cheese scones and sometimes I sit outside the café at one of the picnic tables eating an ice cream.

If you're tired you could take a ride in one of the horse-drawn carriages to the end of the drive. Being a peasant at heart, though, I walked down the drive, along the avenue of lime trees. Swallows were flying so low they skimmed the grass, and I came at a slightly slower pace past the old stone cider press and thatched lodge to swing left down into the centre of the village again.

Opposite the place in the Square where the carriages gather I went into the picnic area of the Mill Café and on up the path between the flower beds to the pub.

The Drum Inn has a lot of style from its dark thatched roof and handsome windows to the white walls and weathered brown brick base. In 1996, the managers celebrated the Drum's Diamond Jubilee.

The inn was built in 1936, with the famous Sir Edwin Lutyens as architect. He, of course, is remembered for his modern masterpiece, Liverpool Cathedral, but as a Devonian I'm more impressed by what he gave us at Cockington.

Since his day changes have been made at the Drum to accommodate changes in pub life and society as a whole. But it's still the local, where tourists and villagers meet. The staff are helpful and cheerful.

In the bars you'll find wooden furniture, little snugs and alcoves, and big open fires. There's a Family Area, woodbeamed ceilings and a restaurant. The lights are soft, and if the atmosphere is pleasantly dim this is no reflection on the locals.

There is a selection of international wines, two real ales – Dartmoor Best and Dartmoor Legend – and among other drinks, draught Guinness. And that's what I had – a tall glass of the 'Plain' with a creamy vicar's collar on it.

Outside, in the sunny beer garden, I lowered the level of the Liffey water and discovered that the jackdaws had taken a fancy to me. If not, why did one of the little rascals place a deposit on my head as I sat there thinking nice thoughts?

4: LANES, MEADOWS AND ALE

IT WAS lunchtime when I arrived at the Harvest Moon, a fine looking, one storey modern pub that stands beside Grange Road in Goodrington. If it's tucked away go and find it – you won't be disappointed.

That's what I did on a perfect summer day of heatwave and hazy blue sky. But if you park in the pub's big car park, please tell the proprietor what you're doing and that the walk ends inside the Harvest Moon.

Torbay had that South of France sun appeal when I turned left out of the car park and came along Grange Road to the old farmworkers' cottages on the bend where it was left again into Ladder Lane.

This was one of my dad's nature trails back in the rare old times, and now that he and mum have opened a pub in paradise, walking the family footpaths has its poignant moments. But the hedges were high and happy sounds filtered through the one hiding the holiday camp.

Wherever the sun shone through the branches and leaves little clouds of gnats whirled about. The bees were less neurotic among the trailing bindweed, goose grass, pennywort and nettles.

Then the lane narrowed to a stony track beyond the toy bridge over a toy stream and climbed the hill to become another of those 'tunnels of green gloom' which well-heeled, romantic poets were always celebrating in those distant summers when life moved at a more leisurely pace.

At the top I was happy to climb the stile and swing in a wide arc to walk the shorn meadows towards Clennon Woods and the downhill section to Clennon Ponds. En route I could look across the sports field to the Leisure Centre, Dartmouth Road, and the bay.

Beyond the gate at the bottom of the final meadow I turned left to stroll around Top Pond. Young birds cried from the buddleia and willow, and winged insects were busy above the horsetails and cow parsley. Horsetails, by the way, are primitive, spore-bearing plants which look like pale green loo brushes.

Up under the woodland trees the Zoo Pond is a brown backwater. Dragonflies tacked across it, grabbing airborne snacks, while luckier pondlife 'blinked' from the surface.

Then I was swinging right, onto the cropped turf of the sports field alongside the low fence of the 'conservation area' and its saplings, flowering grasses and thistles. Grasshoppers zithered and three butterflies were on the wing, a marbled white and a pair of gatekeepers.

A few yards later I bore right to cross the 'isthmus' where mallard and other wildfowl were waiting to be fed by their human regulars. They hardly gave me a glance as I went by and turned left to come along the path beside Middle and Bottom Ponds.

There the dragonfly drama was in full swing, the cygnets, coot and moorhen chicks looked cute, and ducklings gathered round their mothers. Willows, alder, rushes and reeds rustled in the sea breeze and the path was littered with feathers and down.

A lot of flapping and quacking was going on out among the little islands and half-drowned willows, and the gull clamour never let up. But a lot of adult ducks were resting on the edge of Bottom Pond where water poured through the sluice into the stream.

Temperatures were soaring, but a little beyond the last pond the path carried me into the welcome shade of Stuggy Lane. And soon the wider sections gave way to narrows between nettles, cow parsley, tall bushy hedges and chirring crickets.

Grange Court Holiday Camp was on the right, with the golf driving range to the left.

Then the gate opened onto Grange Road and the Harvest Moon was straight ahead, about 300 yards as the gull flies.

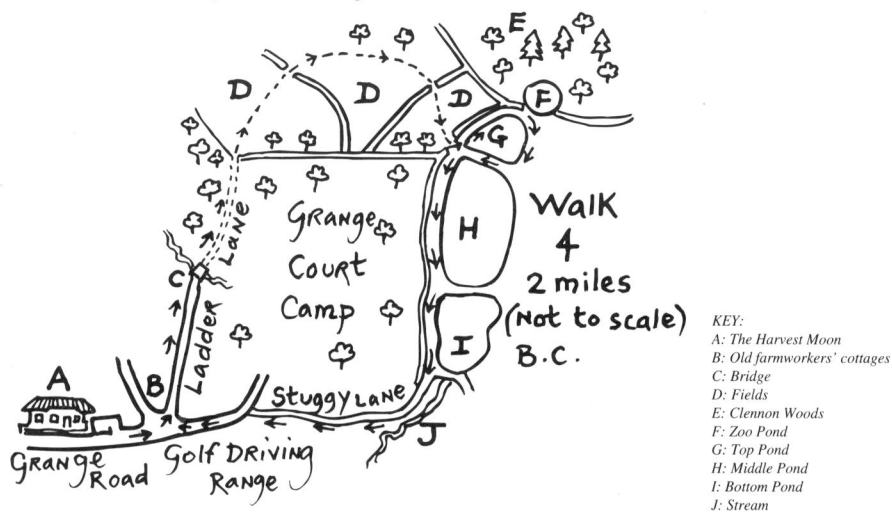

KEY:
A: The Harvest Moon
B: Old farmworkers' cottages
C: Bridge
D: Fields
E: Clennon Woods
F: Zoo Pond
G: Top Pond
H: Middle Pond
I: Bottom Pond
J: Stream

This is a spotlessly clean pub that has moved with the times and has a pleasant relaxed atmosphere which puts strangers at their ease.

Nursing a cool half of Directors ale I had a browse around. The Harvest Moon has polished wood panelling, a bar where two traditional ales are available, along with the usual selection of beers, and a wine list that includes champagne.

It was good to be outside sipping ale, on one of those afternoons the Tourist Board pray for. Nearby, families sat on the grass of the natural picnic area or at picnic tables in the garden. The pub caters for all generations, and the family games room is popular with parents and children.

I topped up my glass and sat there while bees droned around the hanging flower baskets and other floral displays, and swifts screamed through the sunlight of Waterside.

5: PROMS, SUGAR AND BOGART

AS PUBS go, the Inn on the Green is handsome, inside and out. You can't miss its cream façade, there on Paignton seafront, opposite the pier.

And the proprietors employ one of the best parking fee strategies I know. Drivers part with three quid and get the usual windscreen sticker plus a three pound voucher which they can use in the pub for food or drink.

Anyway, leaving the main entrance I crossed Esplanade Road and the Green to turn right and walk along the prom past the Festival Theatre.

The tide was high and the beach was packed. Out in the bay Thatcher Rock and Ore Stone were catching the sun off Torquay's Hope's Nose. A lot of bare feet slapped on the hot pavements as another scorcher brought the tourists flocking to the seaside.

At the end of the prom I swung left and came below the thatched cottages and under the arch to Paignton Harbour. Before me was the familiar, shallow-water harbour scene of small craft at their moorings

Walking on past the Pier Inn I took in the salty cameos as I did when I was a 'tacker' back in the summers of the 1940s. Then, a little beyond the far side of the harbour, it was left turn into Cliff Road and the short walk to the entrance of Roundham Head Park, there on the left at the bend, near the bleak-looking apartment block.

From the footpath over the Head the views were terrific, helped by the clear blue sky and a dark blue sparkling sea. To the left was Hope's Nose and to the right Berry Head, with Tor Bay in between.

The low red cliffs of Paignton ran up against Brixham's limestone, gulls soared high and I came on to the hanging Cliff Gardens for a path and steps descent to the prom and Goodrington South Sands.

It was all choppy, sundazzle water, the beach lost to the tide, the prom crowded with sunbathers and kids splashing about in the shallows.

Refuelling on an ice cream at North Sands kiosk I had a look across Goodrington Park to the lakes and the boating activity before strolling to the Inn on the Quay.

The pub stands on the little headland above Middle Stone – the mussel rocks that separate Goodrington North and South sands. The smoke from the barbecue

Looking down on Paignton Harbour and Roundham Head

grill on the front lawn half hid the queue and I was passing the shops, flumes, carousels and dodgems of Quaywest Water Park.

One of the steam trains bound for Kingswear from Paignton puffed along the Railway above South Sands prom and with more beach showing, the holiday crowds were getting their money's worth.

Roundham Head

On another day, with the tide lower, I could have walked the edge of the wavebreak looking at the marine creatures from crabs to sandworms. But the prom was fine and the Punch and Judy show, the sunshades and pedalos reminded me of school holiday scenes in the bucket-and-spade era.

At the end of the prom I went down the steps and up under the railway bridge to find the footpath signposted on the left. So I came up between the railway, the holiday camp and the bungalow gardens to walk across another railway bridge onto the cropped grass of Three Beaches Head, which has a lot of good picnic spots.

An aerial view which shows Saltern Cove on the left

The footpath on the right led down to Saltern Cove. By the way, these little coves, inlets and promontories, between Churston Point and Corbyn Head are one long Site of Special Scientific Interest.

Saltern Cove is worth a visit if you're interested in marine life. Spider crabs, pipe fish and conger eels live in the big kelp beds, and the rock pools provide close-ups of snake-locks anemones, shrimps, blennies, shore crabs and starfish. And there's lots more for young nature detectives, including close encounters with devil's crabs and their big red eyes.

But at high tide I decided to give the oyster catchers, sea lettuce and red weeds a miss and continue my footpath 'trek' to the Sugar Loaf. This is a grassy dome, a hill in miniature providing great views, seawards and inland across Paignton's green suburbs.

A brief sit-down to read a few of Edward Thomas' poems and I was ready to retrace my steps for a new set of views while the sun honed my thirst to a fine edge.

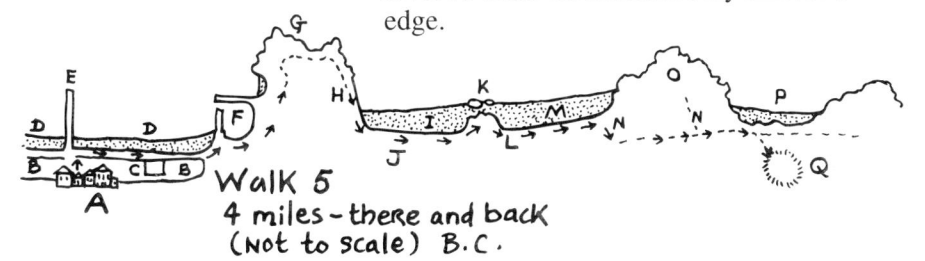

KEY:
A: The Inn on the Green
B: Paignton Green
C: The Festival Theatre
D: Paignton Beach
E: Paignton Pier
F: Paignton Harbour
G: Roundham Head
H: Cliff Gardens
I: Goodrington North Sands
J: Goodrington Park
K: Middle Stone
L: Quaywest Water Park
M: Goodrington South Sands
N: Railway bridge
O: Three Beaches Head
P: Saltern Cove
Q: The Sugar Loaf

Walk 5
4 miles - there and back
(not to scale) B.C.

Pub Walks In and Around Torbay   19

Goodrington Sands

Back at the Inn on the Green it was a relief to get out of the sun into the classy, comfortable pub which has featured on BBC Television's *Breakfast Time* and ITV's *Wish You Were Here*. With that family-friendly atmosphere it's easy to see why the inn had received 'Paignton Best' Awards in consecutive years.

The tables on the seafront sun terrace were all taken, but I was happy to swig away at a pint of Irish Stout in the Bogart Bar before looking around the big interior with its up-market decor and service that came with a smile.

Framed black and white photo studies of Bogie hang in the bar that bears his name, and the rugged old smoothie's "Here's looking at you, kid" whispered through the sort of half-dark that lovers love.

Then I wandered off to run a drinker's nose over the scene. Among the real ales were Theakston's XB, and the wine list peaked to Bollinger. But the lagers were equally impressive, the ciders on tap were OK and my pint of Beamish tasted great. The background music was just right and it would have taken a long time to have read the menu.

Adventurous as ever I had farmhouse cheese and pickle sandwiches before browsing to look at the Theatre Bar, which lays on live entertainment; the Family Room with its kids' disco and large screen video; and the sun terrace.

If the Inn on the Green features in most Good Pub Guides you can put it down to the vision of the owners and the efforts of the staff. Like the man said: "Here's looking at you, kid."

6: SERENADED BY THE GRASSHOPPER CHORUS

WHEN you arrive at the Barton Pines ask the owners if you can leave the car in their car park while you do the walk, and tell them you'll pop in afterwards to sample the hospitality.

Leaving the car park late one sunny morning I turned right into West Lane, putting Blagdon Road behind me. Then, on the left opposite the modern buildings of Hunter's Court, I paused to enjoy the gateway view of the countryside.

Low, rolling hills, covered in green pastures, yellow and brown cornfields, patches of red soil and dark green woods, ran to Tor Bay with Berry Head on the horizon.

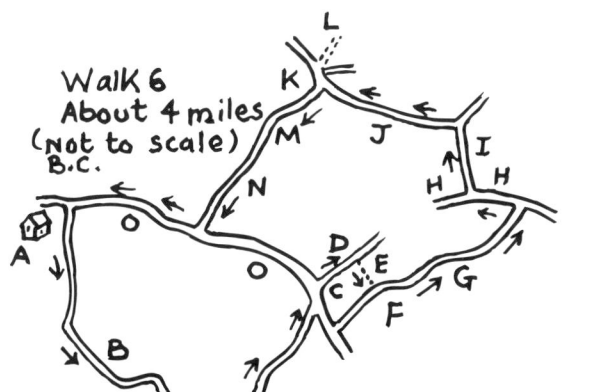

KEY:
A: Barton Pines Inn
B: West Lane
C: The Old Poundhouse
D: Middle Blagdon Lane
E: Footpath
F: Lower Blagdon
G: Lower Blagdon Lane
H: Middle Blagdon Lane
I: Middle Ramshill Lane
J: Old Widdicombe
K: Buttshill Cross
L: Beacon Hill
M: Butts Hill
N: Higher Blagdon
O: Blagdon Road

The sky was full of house martins, tearing about and bleeping at each other against the big white clouds. It was Devon with 'glorious' parked in front of it, and the crickets and grasshoppers in the hedge bottoms couldn't stop zithering.

Walking on I put up a yellowhammer from a bank covered in field bindweed, while butterflies of all colours fluttered through the sunlight between the hedges.

Farmwork was going on in the wayside yard and I came down the long hill, around the bend into the combe. But soon it was uphill beyond another bend as I caught a new set of landscape views.

Serenaded by the hopper and cricket chorus I reached the hill top for the gentle descent to Blagdon Road. After making sure no traffic was approaching, I nipped across and swung right at The Old Poundhouse to walk down Middle Blagdon Lane past old walls, old properties, old orchards and some fairly new barn conversions. And there was the footpath on the right, opposite the iron gate of Old Barn House.

It was great to climb the stile, get out of the heat and stroll in the shade beside the stream which brought me to Lower Blagdon.

In Lower Blagdon Lane I turned left to walk the steep hill past a row of thatched cottages.

Cloud shadows ghosted over the farmland and I had just the butterflies for company on yet another long, but attractive, uphill slog.

At the top, a lot of red soil gleamed in a field and I loped down to the crossroads before turning left into Middle Blagdon Lane for the switchback walking to the next cross.

Here I swung right and saw the two tall masts standing on Beacon Hill.

Presently Middle Ramshill Lane provided a lovely gate view over standing corn, looking towards the South Hams. Uphill all the way, it was left again at the next Cross to climb even higher along the lane called Old Widdicombe.

Not far from the yard full of tyres I was at Buttshill Cross and Higher Blagdon was there below. So I made a very sharp left turn and came down Butts Hill under the wood past the old sandstone barn, the sandstone cottages, the hedge of vines, Orchard House and Rose Cottage, to the farm.

The corner of the field by the farmhouse was full of white geese and their cries followed me to the old well-house, where I turned right and came carefully up Blagdon Road, watching out for the traffic.

Set among the tall trees which give it its name, Barton Pines was built in 1892 as a private residence. And although it's popular with summer visitors it's also a local in the rural tradition.

Coming in out of the noon sun I had a look round the big bar. The style is Elizabethan, the panelling is wood and the ceilings are high. Yet the place had a snug feel to it.

The wooden furniture helped create the sort of atmosphere both novice and veteran drinkers appreciate. But I also liked the old fashioned jukebox, the darts board in the corner, the Jamesons and Scottish malts, and the Kilkenny Irish beer, but there was a wide range of beers and lagers.

At Barton Pines they cater, too, for the younger palate, with Bacardi breezers, Budweiser, Becks and Holstein also available.

The holiday camp, open air swimming pool and holiday flats are part of the country complex centred on the inn. And the pub facilities include a family room, skittle alley and a couple of pool tables, a children's playground complete with Mother Hubbard slide and climbing frame, and a non-smoking dining area for all the family.

Alas, I was steering clear of alcohol till the evening and after a fried breakfast fit for even Rab C. Nesbitt, wasn't even peckish. But it was enough to wander outside and sample once more the view over the summer fields to the sea.

7: SEASIDE CAPPUCCINO BUT NO SIGN OF BARDOT

TORQUAY harbourside was crowded and not many of the tables outside Vaughan's Continental Bar were empty. The sun beat down and both sea and sky were hazy blue, as I headed for the narrows beyond the Wallace Arnold office.

Vaughan's is on Vaughan Parade, one of the quays of the inner harbour, with views across the water to some of the town's hillside highrises, the clock tower and The Strand.

That morning was all go, from the cormorants diving among the boats to the bustle on the quay and in the cafés. To be honest, the heat was stifling and I envied the seabirds splashing about between the moored launches and pleasure craft.

Round the corner was Torquay Marina and on my right stood the Pavilion shopping centre. Now the prom was broad enough for the world's biggest Samurai to have marched along it 12 abreast. But I had a browse around the flowerbeds and fountains of Princess Gardens on my way to the Princess Theatre and the pier.

Walk 7
About 2 miles
(not to scale)
B.C.

KEY:
A: Vaughan's Continental Bar
B: The Strand
C: The Harbour
D: Torquay Marina
E: Pavilion shopping centre
F: Princess Theatre
G: A379 Torbay Road
H: Abbey Sands
I: Corbyn Sands
J: Harbreck Rock
K: Corbyn's Head
L: Torre Abbey
M: English Riviera Centre

It's worth strolling along the pier. You'll get glimpses of some of Tor Bay's marine life and can watch the anglers hauling in the mackerel.

Then the prom took me past the Tropicana restaurant with views across the bay to Corbyn's Head. The coastline beyond was lost in the sea mist but this only served to lend a touch of mystery.

If the bay was hazy, the water was clear and I could look over the handrail into the shallows. Abbey Sands is typical of Torbay's many safe family beaches. And a lot of holidaymakers were enjoying the sun and the sea as I padded along the prom. If the tide hadn't been in I might have taken to the edge of it to see what the waves had churned up, you know, things like shellfish and starfish.

On the right was the busy A379 Torbay Road with the parkland of Torre Abbey above it, and the English Riviera Centre prominent not far from the mansion. Both the Abbey and the Centre deserve a visit, but my destination was Corbyn's Head. In any case, as a local, I'm familiar with most of Torbay's landmarks.

The going was good and soon, coming up the gentle slope above Corbyn Sands, where I could have stopped for a cool drink or an ice cream, I was opposite the Grand Hotel.

On the Head the lawns were cropped in fashionable macho style and there were public lavatories. If the mist had cleared there would also have been great bay views but I was content with the sea smells and the rising breeze, which took some of the heaviness out of the air.

Dolphins often come into Tor Bay but not that day. So I made my way back along the prom towards a blurred vision of Torquay and its hillside villas, hotels and apartment blocks.

By the time I had reached Vaughan's Bar the lunchtime trade was keeping the staff on their toes. Couples and family groups sat outside at the tables under parasols, and the barmaids dispensing the drinks had that cheerful continental fizz about them.

In the mornings it's teas and coffees, when Vaughan's attracts a lot of senior citizens. Then, at lunchtime, families come in for meals, and in the evening youngsters and families share the bar.

Families are welcome to sit where they like and enjoy food cooked to order or the menu meals, bottled beers, ciders, wines, soft drinks or continental coffees.

The wine list is long, and the lagers will please most palates, ranging as they

Torre Abbey, close to the seafront

do from Becks to Carlsberg Ice with its six-plus alcoholic Richter reading, but the bar does stock spirits.

Yes, the atmosphere and the drinks had a definite continental flavour, which I liked. Age didn't come into it. The young, the mature and the vintage can blend as they did in the past; and, mulling over my student days in Paris a few years before rock and roll hit the scene, I sipped a Vaughan's cappuccino, wondering why Bardot was late.

8: WALKING DOWN INTO THE VALLEY OF THE ROCKS

MAIDENCOMBE is on the far northern rural fringe of Torbay, a quiet little community on the hillsides and in the combe above the sea cliffs.

Setting off from the public car park I headed north towards the Thatched Tavern, which was there on the right at the bend which swung me left past houses and old farm buildings to the Courthouse opposite the cider apple orchard.

It was mid-morning on a roasting hot day of a few scattered high clouds, the usual insect zither and the dark green foliage of late August.

The Courthouse is about 600 years old and in the garden stands the celebrated Judas Tree, imported as a sapling from Lebanon around 1550, and lovely to look at in the spring.

The bottom part of Steep Hill carried me up the combe to Rockhouse Lane where the banks were high and scarred with badger runs, and the hedges were among the tallest I've seen. They met in the middle to form a great arch of leaves.

Rudyard Kipling, who lived in Rockhouse Lane during the last century, would have taken this route to the sea or maybe settled for the path signposted Watcombe, which I took at the bend a little beyond Brim Hill.

This provided pleasant strolling alongside the clifftop woods and meadows, and wonderful sea views.

The twisting, turning switchback brought me to the top of the Goat Path, with an alcove and bench among the bushes on the left. The path is a rough track running along the foot of a cliff covered in all sorts of plants like the wild onion, wild carrot and wild cabbage, marjoram and valerian.

Over the treetops to the left were more sea pictures and the cries of seabirds and songbirds mingled in comic stereophonic.

Presently I was at the bottom of what was once the Sunday Cream Tea Trail which my grandparents' generation had taken from Watcombe to Maidencombe back in the Rare Old Times. A wood of mature sycamores provided the shade and I was walking a path of red mud through the Valley of the Rocks among the old pits where terracotta clay was once quarried.

Then the gleaming red buttress of Giant Rock towered above the trees and I stopped to look up at the fantastic sandstone crag which is Torquay's Yosemite. Tarzan might have found the creepers hanging from the face attractive but the local jackdaws, jangling away were eager to tell me this really was South Devon and not South America.

The Goat Path

The Valley of the Rocks is a good picnic area, but I came back up the Goat Path to the bench at the top where I took the coastal path signposted sharp right. And this saw me through some wild woodland onto the track that followed the edge of the fields into cirl bunting territory.

The rough pasture and high hedges offer ideal habitat for this rare little songbird. Nearly all the 300 pairs breeding in the UK are in South Devon and some of them favour Maidencombe.

As usual, though, I didn't see any and didn't hear the telltale trilling rattle. Then I climbed a flight of rough steps and came through a gap in the rock cut by quarrymen and bore right at the next path junction.

This ran between the bunting meadows and clifftop woodland, conjuring up encounters with butterflies, bees, songbird fledgelings, grasshoppers and fellow ramblers.

By now I knew how hot dogs felt under the grill, but back in the car park the pub proved more attractive than nearby Maidencombe Beach.

So off I went to the Thatched Tavern.

The pub has plenty of customer appeal, from its award-winning garden and the

Cottage Restaurant, to the bar and main restaurant. The owners have cultivated a fine cottage atmosphere, a pub in the traditional style with no gimmicks. Good food, drink, service and the right setting are what the customer gets here.

The Main Restaurant is charming, and to reach the Cottage Restaurant I descended some steps into a cosy corner that has an open fire in the winter.

There is a large choice of wines, spirits and beers on offer. The spirit list includes some good malts and the Irish Black Bush and Jamesons. The beers range from Dartmoor Ale, Bass and Caffreys, to draught Guinness and Carlsberg Export. Cider is limited to Blackthorn Dry.

If I'd been indulging in an evening session, under the low, beamed ceiling, I'd have gone for the Caffreys and Guinness, with Black Bush chasers. But the wine list is extensive, climbing from Semillon Chardonnay to Cuvée Louis Domier, brut champagne.

Most folk visiting the Thatched Tavern come for the food, sampling house specialities. Anyway, customers were coming in as I headed for the garden to sit under the big, spreading chestnut tree with a Gaelic Irish whiskey coffee for company.

The two cats that joined me belong to the pub chefs. The fluffy black one was Blacky and the sleek black one was Sooty, or maybe sauté, remembering its owner's job!

But the Thatched Tavern garden, with its wishing well, flowers, cats and tree, is as memorable as the pub itself, and a delightful place to end a stroll.

KEY:
A: The Thatched Tavern
B: Maidencombe Beach
C: Car park
D: Steep Hill
E: Brim Hill
F: Rockhouse Lane
G: Fields
H: The Goat Path
I: Watcombe Beach
J: Old terracotta pits
K: Giant Rock
L: Car park
M: Beach Road
N: Valley of the Rocks

Walk 8
About 3 miles
(Not to scale)
B.C.

9: UP ON THE DOWNS

SO LONG as you let the manager know you'll be a customer at the end of the walk you can park at the rear of the Inn. But please do have the courtesy to finish the stroll with a drink or something to eat.

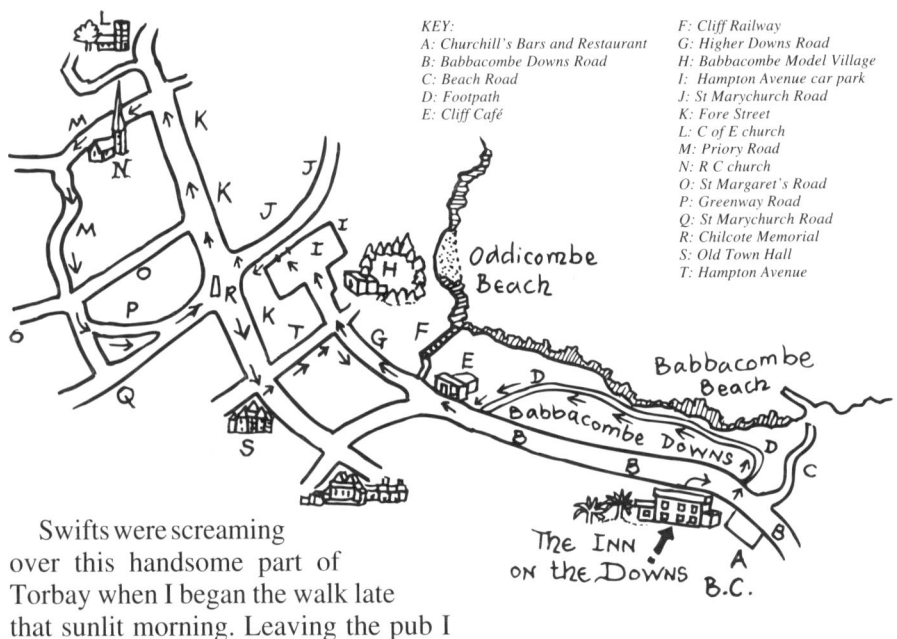

KEY:
A: Churchill's Bars and Restaurant
B: Babbacombe Downs Road
C: Beach Road
D: Footpath
E: Cliff Café
F: Cliff Railway
G: Higher Downs Road
H: Babbacombe Model Village
I: Hampton Avenue car park
J: St Marychurch Road
K: Fore Street
L: C of E church
M: Priory Road
N: R C church
O: St Margaret's Road
P: Greenway Road
Q: St Marychurch Road
R: Chilcote Memorial
S: Old Town Hall
T: Hampton Avenue

Swifts were screaming over this handsome part of Torbay when I began the walk late that sunlit morning. Leaving the pub I turned right and crossed Babbacombe Downs Road at Churchill's to come left along the clifftop path.

As 'seafronts' go this one is really impressive, with Channel views other holiday resorts can only envy. Green fields and woods sloped to the edge of red cliffs that run all the way to Dawlish. But the coast beyond the Exe estuary was hidden by a thin sea mist that was slowly rising.

Lyme Bay was a perfect summer blue, gulls wheeled and wailed, and yachts with limp sails drifted in the sort of breeze that would have struggled to ruffle a hamster's fur.

A lot of folk were taking the sun on the benches or in deckchairs, on the lawns between flowerbeds and palm trees. The flags on the flagpoles hardly stirred and I was glared at by an old gent who had failed four times to light his cigar with unhelpful matches.

Over the railings on the right, where the cliffs fell a long way to the sea, was that glorious vision of blue meeting blue. To the left, above gently sloping grass, stood the pubs, hotels and restaurants which had once been the villas of the well-off, drawn to this part of England by the weather and the views.

Oddicombe Beach was down below, served by the Cliff Railway which was built in 1926, and a public telescope was at hand for close-ups of the sandstone crag parade. But I had ice cream on my mind, and there, not far from the little statue of Georgina, Baroness Mount-Temple on her fountain, was the Cliff Café.

I often stop there when I'm on a pushbike hike. Everything the holidaymaker or overheated cyclist could want is available, from ice-cold slush, ice creams and cold drinks, to a wide variety of hot or cold snacks.

Licking the blob of vanilla-flavoured soft stuff on a cone, I came along the pavement into Higher Downs Road to walk past the big gardens of big houses to Hampton Avenue car park and the queue outside Babbacombe Model Village. This internationally famous tourist attraction is a must for kids and adults. In fact it's a marvel, with miniature communities, railways, lakes, people and everything else laid out in gardens surrounded by banks of conifers of all shapes, sizes and shades of green.

Walking on across the car park I swung left at the blue information board, then right, over the pedestrian crossing into Fore Street and St Marychurch shopping precinct.

There was a village here in 925 AD and St Marychurch is still a village in atmosphere and spirit. Traffic-free, the top part of Fore

Street is a very pleasant place to shop. A lot of small businesses and traders provide quality goods and you can enjoy a coffee, al fresco, among the flower baskets, old street lamps, trees and tubs of flowers.

After a good browse I turned left into Priory Road and had a look at the elegant Catholic Church of Our Lady and St Denis, whose spire is a familiar Torbay landmark.

Priory Road wound on down past St Catherine's Road. A Flymo snarled and butterflies were sun-dancing in the gardens of more wayside villas. Crossing St Margaret's Road I looked back at the Roman Catholic Church steeple, which shares the skyline with the tower of the Anglican parish Church of St Mary.

Another left turn brought me into Greenway Road and on to Fore Street, below the shopping precinct, where I swung right at the Chilcote Memorial to browse past the shops, the Tudor Café and the railway museum.

St Marychurch Town Hall is a lovely old building and the zebra crossing outside its front door took me safely to the other side of the road and Hampton Avenue. I was sharing the pavement with holidaymakers heading for the Model Village, but turning right opposite Hampton Avenue car park I retraced my steps to another Cliff Café ice cream and that sunny stroll along the high seafront.

Back at the Inn on the Downs the Manager, Mr Russell Clevedon-Powell, and his staff were coping with the brisk lunchtime trade. Waiting my turn I was glad the pub beer garden was exactly that – a grassy garden with shrubs and palm trees where you can relax over a cool drink.

Inside there are two bars – including the Functions Room and restaurant. Master Chef Paul Webb offers tasty bar snacks or more elaborate meals on his Chef's Menu. The restaurant area is delightful and the seating is comfortable. Most beers are available, bottled or draught, and the usual selection of wines and spirits, or Ironoak cider on tap.

Throughout the year Mr Powell lays on live evening entertainment, including Country and Western.

I took my half of lager and sandwich into the garden and sat at a table in the sun, serenaded by a solo bumble bee. Then the local sparrows started Line Dancing on the lawn as part of their 'spare-us-a-crumb, mate' scrounge routine.